Three unaccompanied Part-songs for mixed voices

Edward Elgar

T0084051

CONTENTS

Novello Publishing Limited
14 / 15 Berners Street, London W1T 3LJ
Exclusive distributors: Music Sales Limited,
Newmarket Road, Bury St. Edmunds, Suffolk IP33 3YB

Order No. NOV070437R

TO ALFRED H. LITTLETON

GO, SONG OF MINE

CHORUS *(UNACCOMPANIED)* IN SIX PARTS
THE WORD BY GUIDO CALVACANTI (1250 – 1301)
TRANSLATED BY D. G. ROSETTI
THE MUSIC BY
EDWARD ELGAR
(Op. 57)

song of mine, . . To break the hard - ness
song of mine, . . To break the hard - ness of the heart of man: . .
p dim.
song of mine, . . To break the hard - ness of the heart of man: . .
p dim.
song of mine, . . To break the hard - ness of the heart of man:
p dim.
song of mine, . . To break the hard - ness of the heart of man:
p dim.
song of mine, . . To break the hard - ness of the heart of man: . .
p dim.
ppp
. . . Go, song of mine, ...
ppp
. . . Go, . . song . . . of mine, ...
ppp
. . . Go, . . song . . . of mine, ...
Quasi Recit. molto espress.
p
Go, song of mine, To break . . the hard - ness . . of the heart of
pp dim.
Quasi Recit. molto espress.
p
Go, song of mine, To break . . the hard - ness . . of the heart of
pp dim.
ppp
. . . Go, song of mine, ...
pp

ppp **rit.**

Go, song of mine, ...

ppp **rit.**

Go, . . song . . of mine, ...

ppp **rit.**

Go, . . song . . of mine, ...

p Quasi Recit. molto espress. *distinto, dim. e rit.*

Say how his life be - gan, . . From dust, . . and in that dust doth sink su - pine: . .

p Quasi Recit. molto espress. *distinto, dim. e rit.*

Say how his life be - gan, . . From dust, . . and in that dust doth sink su - pine: . .

ppp **rit.**

Go, song of mine, ...

ppp *dim. e rit.*

Molto sostenuto e cantabile.

p a tempo. *cres.* > *sf ten.* *cres.*

Yet, say, yet, say, th'un-err - ing spi - rit of grief shall guide His soul, shall

p a tempo. *cres.* > *sf* *cres.*

Yet, say, yet, say, th'un-err - ing spi - rit of grief . . shall guide, shall

a tempo. *cres.* > *sf* *cres.*

Yet, say, yet, say, th'un-err - ing spi - rit of grief . . shall guide, shall

p a tempo. *cres.* > *sf* *cres.*

. . . Yet, say, . . th'un - err - ing spi - rit of grief shall guide His soul, shall

p a tempo. *cres.* > *sf* *cres.*

. . . Yet, say, . . th'un - err - ing spi - rit of grief shall guide His soul, shall

p a tempo. *cres.* > *sf*

Yet, say, . . yet, say th'un-err - ing spi - rit of grief shall guide, shall

Molto sostenuto e cantabile.

p a tempo. *cres.* > *sf* *cres.*

Allargando.
ff
espress.
p
guide, shall guide his soul, yet, say, th' un-err - ing spi - rit of grief shall
sf
guide his soul, . . . say, yet, say, th' un-err - ing spi - rit of grief shall
guide his soul, . . . say, yet, say, th'un-err - ing spi - rit of grief shall
guide, shall guide his soul, yet, say, th' un-err - ing spi - rit of grief shall.
guide, shall guide his soul, yet, say, th' un-err - ing spi - rit of grief shall.
guide his soul, yet, . . say, the un - err - - ing spi - rit of
Allargando.
cres.
guide his soul, . . shall guide his soul, be-ing pu - - ri -
legato.
guide, shall guide his soul, shall guide his soul, grief shall guide . .
guide, shall guide his soul, shall guide his soul, be-ing pu - - ri -
. . . guide . . his soul, . . shall guide his soul, be-ing pu- ri-fied, grief shall guide . .
. . . guide . . his soul, . . shall guide his soul, be-ing pu- ri-fied, grief shall guide . .
grief shall guide, . . . shall guide, guide his soul, . . be - ing
ff legato.

ten.
- fi - - ed, . . pu - ri - fi - ed, To seek its Ma - ker at the
. . his soul, be-ing pu - ri - fi - ed, be-ing pu - ri - fied, pu - ri - fied, To
- fi - - - ed, pu - ri - fi - ed, be-ing pu - ri - fied, pu - ri - fied, To
. . his soul, be-ing pu - ri - fi - ed, pu - ri - fi - ed, To
. . his soul, be-ing pu - ri - fi - ed pu - ri - fied, pu - ri - fied, To
pu - ri - fi - ed, pu - ri - fi - ed, be-ing pu - ri - fi - ed, To
pu - ri - fi - ed, be-ing pu - ri - fi - ed, To
heav'n - - - - - - ly, heav'n - - - -
seek its Ma - ker at the heav'n - ly shrine, to seek its Ma - ker at the
seek its Ma - ker at the heav'n - ly shrine, to seek its Ma - ker at the
seek its Ma - ker at . . the heav'n - ly shrine, to seek its Ma - ker at . . the
seek its Ma - ker at the heav'n - ly shrine, to seek its Ma - ker at the
seek its Ma - ker at . . the heav'n - ly shrine, to seek its Ma - ker at . . the
seek its Ma - ker at . . the heav'n - ly shrine, to seek its Ma - ker at . . the

- ly shrine; His

heav'n - ly shrine, to seek its Ma-ker at the heav'n - - ly

heav'n - ly shrine, to seek its Ma-ker at the heav'n - - ly

heav'n - ly shrine, to seek its Ma-ker at the heav'n - - ly

heav'n - ly shrine, to seek its Ma-ker at the heav'n - - ly

heav'n - ly shrine, to seek its Ma-ker at the heav'n - - -

heav'n - ly shrine, to seek its Ma-ker at the heav'n - - -

soul be - ing . . pu - ri - fied . . shall seek its

shrine; The un-err - ing spi-rit of grief shall guide His soul . . to its

shrine; The un-err - ing spi-rit of grief shall guide His soul . . to its

shrine; Th'un-err - ing spi-rit of grief shall guide His soul . . to its

shrine; The un-err - ing spi-rit of grief shall guide His soul . . to its

shrine, ... to seek, ... to seek its

- ly shrine, ... to seek, . . to seek its

(Careggi, 1909.)

HOW CALMLY THE EVENING*

WORDS BY T. T. LYNCH

COMPOSED BY
EDWARD ELGAR

*Composed expressly for *The Musical Times*.

Copyright, 1907, by Novello and Company Limited.

come, our life's work and its brev - i - ty feel - - ing, ..

come, our life's .. work .. and its brev - i - ty feel - - - .

come, our life's work .. and its brev - i - ty feel - - - .

come, our life's work and its brev - i - ty feel - - - .

. . With thanks for the past, for the fu - ture we pray.

ing, . . . With thanks for the past, for the fu - ture we pray.

- ing, . . With thanks for the past, for the fu - ture we pray.

- ing, . . With thanks for the past, for the fu - ture we pray.

Lord, save us from fol - ly; be with us in sor - row; . . . Sus-tain us in

Lord, save us from fol - ly; be . . with us in sor - row; Sus - tain . . us in

Lord, save us from fol - ly; be . . with us in sor - row; Sus - tain . . us in

Lord, save us from fol - ly; be with us in sor - row; . . . Sus-tain us in

work . till the time of our rest, ... the time of our

work till the time . . of our rest, . . . the time of our

work till the time . . of our rest, . . . the time of our

work till the time . . of our rest, . . . the time of our

rest; .. When earth's day is o - ver, may hea - ven's to - mor - row.

rest; .. When earth's day is o - ver, may hea - ven's to - mor - - -

rest; .. When earth's day is .. o - ver, may hea - ven's to - mor - -

rest; .. When earth's day is o - ver, may hea - ven's to - mor - -

. . . Dawn on us, of homes long ex - pect - ed pos - sest. . .

- row . . Dawn on us, of homes long .. ex - pect - ed pos - sest. . .

- row . . Dawn on us, of homes long .. ex - pect - ed pos - sest. . .

- row . . Dawn on us, of homes long .. ex - pect - ed pos - sest. . .

GOOD MORROW

(A SIMPLE CAROL FOR HIS MAJESTY'S HAPPY RECOVERY)

First performed by the Choir of St. George's Chapel, Windsor Castle,
at their Annual Concert, December 9th 1929

WORDS FROM GEORGE GASCOIGNE

MUSIC BY
EDWARD ELGAR

N.B. In programmes the words should be printed as on p.24

cresc.
breaks your sleeps, Or do - lours do dis - tress; Yet bear a part in dole-ful wise,
cresc.
dis - tress; Yet bear a part in dole-ful wise,
cresc.
breaks your sleeps, Or do - lours do dis - tress; Yet bear a part in dole-ful wise,
cresc.
breaks your sleeps, Or do - lours do dis - tress; Yet bear a part in dole-ful wise,
cresc.
mf
Yea, think it good ac - cord And an ac-cept-a-ble sac - ri-fice, Each
mf
Yea, think it good ac - cord And an ac-cept-a-ble sac - ri-fice, Each
mf
Yea, think it good ac - cord And an ac-cept-a-ble sac - ri-fice, Each
mf
Yea, think it good ac - cord And an ac-cept-a-ble sac - ri-fice, Each
mf
pp legato e dolce
sprite to praise the Lord. The lit-tle birds which sing so sweet Are
pp legato e dolce
sprite to praise the Lord. The lit-tle birds which sing so sweet, so
sprite to praise the Lord.
sprite to praise the Lord.
pp legato

*Sing the small notes when unaccompanied

GOODE MORROWE

Words from George Gascoigne (1540 – 1578?)
Music by EDWARD ELGAR

(A SIMPLE CAROL FOR HIS MAJESTY'S HAPPY RECOVERY)

1. You that have spent the silent night
   In sleepe and quiet rest,
   And joye to see the cheerefull lyght
   That ryseth in the East:
   Now cleare your voyce, and chere your hart,
   Come helpe me nowe to sing:
   Eche willing wight, come beare a part,
   To prayse the heavenly King.

2. And you whome care in prison keepes,
   Or sickenes doth suppresse,
   Or secret sorrowe breakes your sleepes,
   Or dolours doe distresse:
   Yet beare a parte in dolfull wise,
   Yea, thinke it good accorde
   And an acceptable sacrifice,
   Eche sprite to prayse the lorde.

3. The little byrdes which sing so swete,
   Are like the angelles voyce,
   Which render God his prayses meete,
   And teache us to rejoyce:
   And as they more esteeme that myrth
   Than dread the nights anoy,
   So much we deeme our days on earth,
   But hell to heavenly joye.

4. Unto which Joyes for to attayne
   God graunt us all his grace,
   And sende us after worldly payne,
   In heaven to have a place.
   Where we maye still enjoye that light
   Which never shall decaye:
   Lorde for thy mercy lend us might
   To see that joyfull daye.

5. The Rainbowe bending in the skye,
   Bedeckte with sundrye hewes,
   Is like the seate of God on hye,
   And seemes to tell these newes:
   That as thereby he promisèd,
   To drowne the world no more,
   So by the bloud which Christ hath shead,
   He will our helth restore.

ISBN 0-85360-566-1

EXCLUSIVELY
DISTRIBUTED BY
HAL LEONARD
CORPORATION
14033585
U.S. $9.00